ETERNAL
ENERGY
——AND——
INFORMATION

JIMMY NINJA CHAIKONG

BALBOA.PRESS
A DIVISION OF HAY HOUSE

Balboa Press books may be ordered through booksellers or by contacting:

Balboa Press
A Division of Hay House
1663 Liberty Drive
Bloomington, IN 47403
www.balboapress.com
844-682-1282

Because of the dynamic nature of the Internet, any web addresses or links contained in this book may have changed since publication and may no longer be valid. The views expressed in this work are solely those of the author and do not necessarily reflect the views of the publisher, and the publisher hereby disclaims any responsibility for them.

The author of this book does not dispense medical advice or prescribe the use of any technique as a form of treatment for physical, emotional, or medical problems without the advice of a physician, either directly or indirectly. The intent of the author is only to offer information of a general nature to help you in your quest for emotional and spiritual well-being. In the event you use any of the information in this book for yourself, which is your constitutional right, the author and the publisher assume no responsibility for your actions.

Any people depicted in stock imagery provided by Getty Images are models, and such images are being used for illustrative purposes only. Certain stock imagery © Getty Images.

Print information available on the last page.

ISBN: 978-1-9822-5275-5 (sc)
ISBN: 978-1-9822-5276-2 (e)

Balboa Press rev. date: 08/19/2020

CONTENTS

I've been waiting for some time to begin my book. I don't know why. Perhaps I needed time to mature to a level where I had something original to say. I have created a lot of projects in my time from songs, art, techniques for gymnastics, martial arts, stories, inventions etc. yet nothing I have ever considered unique or an original thought… till now.

I spent my whole life searching for meaning and living my science as a field study of life. I have earned numerous degrees in several disciplines which have only introduced me to new things that I now have more questions than answers for. Yet at this point in my 40 years I have observed a few original ideas I think are worth sharing.

I would like to thank all of my teachers, coaches, friends, songwriters and crazies that I have met along the way that have influenced my life and my story and self image of who it is I am.

CHAPTER ONE

The Science of Human Interaction & Energy

Have you ever noticed when pool balls strike together and play off one another and find a way to bank off each other to find themselves in their goal, the hole? I have and people are very much the same. We bounce off of one another, reflecting and deflecting each others energy as we go thru life creating our little romances and battles with each and every person we encounter from the waiter to the girlfriend to the minister to the father to the mother to the brother to the barber to the student and to the teacher. Still don't get it? Ok here is an example:

Man, let's call him Jim wakes up in a foul mood, his wife Christies is in a good mood making breakfast, Jim comes out does his angry dance, Christie then "decides" Jim you are offending me with your foul mood I am now upset and when I go to my first meeting with my hairdresser Jane I will pass my tale of pissed offness to her and the cycle of negativity will continue, hence one ball banging into the next effecting the next creating a possibility of where the day will end. However this is not a set standard, we (humans) are the variable because Christie could have also been spending time listening to her Abraham- Hicks Affirmations or reading her Eckart Tolle affirmation Calendar and when Jim came in with his Foul Mood she deflected his negativity with a lesson in patience or acceptance or self-realization that Jim's foul mood is his own responsibility and I will not take part in it with him and therefore disconnecting the energy flow that was going to sink the eight ball. This energy dynamic can be witnessed in everyday life. See for yourself. Many people walk around wondering why they feel a certain way or why their day is going so badly or so good. The reason unless you are self aware and setting and resetting your own tempo at multiple times you are probably one of these balls that are banged around by the cue ball. I however seek to be the cue ball because that is the ball setting the tempo for the game or life or if you haven't been following this analogy the way we inner act with one another. This is so interesting if you realize the game is predicted by your ability to play it, so is life.

GAWD

I say God like that; the way old time preacher's pronounces it because it draws a parallel between my version of Gawd and the average view of the mythological God.

I was born in Thailand and I came to the United States when I was very young. Buddhism is the national religion of Thailand and My Mothers 1st religion. When we 1st moved to Texas my mother was married to a G.I. that left her after she stabbed him 9 times for slapping me off a table one night and knocking out my front teeth when he came home in a drunken stupor. After that, speaking very little English we needed help and somehow or another someone from Elmcrest Baptist Church started coming around to help this woman and her young son with food and just general assistance living in a foreign country. The trade off was we were now Baptist! What a fascinating story, Jesus of Nazareth Born in a Manger, Disappears at 13 after a remarkable visit to the temple to astound Wise men with his knowledge, shows back up at Thirty to defy the Jerusalem Jewish Hierarchy and Roman Empire to die a Horrible a Death that sets all men free who accept him as their lord and savior and shapes most of western civilization for the next 3,000 years. Great Story huh? One problem, where's the proof for any of these things that have anything to do with anything relevant to my life today. Not only that where did Jesus go after he was 13 and why isn't any of that documented? I have read many books that say at the age of 12 or 13 when a Jewish male is bar mitzvah they are declared a Man and it is time for them to marry and Jesus being the intellect he was did not want to marry and ran away to the east, so far east that he traveled thru much of India and Asia where he was heavily influenced by the teachings of someone who preceded him by about 500 years The Buddha. The East Greatest Spiritual Teacher had crossed paths with Jesus of Nazareth or more likely one of Buda's disciples at one of the many of Buddhist monasteries along the way. So now Jesus finished with his travels and missing his mother, what boy doesn't miss his mother returns to the Holy Land with all this newfound knowledge in the healing arts, Reiki, acupuncture, hypnosis, meditation, philosophy etc...Comes back preaching a new revolution and turns the Jewish establishment on its head. His charisma, stories and courage to stand up to the "Man" makes him a Hero to the disenfranchised youth of the times and starts a Revolution. Not that I believe this tale either, because where is the proof for any of these mythologies. All stories have some Truth to them like Zeus and the Greek gods and Romans could have once been based on real characters in the human timeline. However most of these stories are depictions or word of mouth or scrolls written hundreds of years after the actual event occurred. If I were to be born a thousand years from now and find the book green eggs and ham am I to believe there was such a character as Sam I Am and he had issues with people eating his hen and pig products? I happen to think eggs and ham are delicious yet it doesn't mean that I will believe any old story attached to them. So my point is I was told a lot of Beautiful Mythologies about a God and his word and his disciples and his desires for my life and I came to find that after all of my study of science, archeology, philosophy and the other world religions that there is no substantial proof for God. I have had what I consider to be a Conversation with God since I was very young yet could this be my higher consciousness or maybe just an over active creative imagination? I don't know and I cannot prove it no matter how much I believe in my own beliefs yet I am humble enough to admit that I might not know what I think I know. Yet that's ok, who Sais we have to have it all figured out? I don't believe we have to know everything, especially things that cannot be proved and especially when there are so many things that science has to share with us that can be proven that will take a lifetime just to observe.

The one thing that has always perplexed me though however is synchronistic events. Many times in my life things have added up, the right people at the right time, the right opportunity at the right time. This and music and the "Magic" behind science are where I find my Gawd. I do not believe in a mythological Creator however I do Believe in the Creator that Creates thru the Physics it Created. If the voice I hear in my head is not Gawd I accept it as my higher self which can weed thru all the bullshit and lead me to my highest good and better decisions. What I sense and what I think might be going on in the Universe is irrelevant to the fact that I am alive, I am seeking my own Truth and will not accept someone else's Truth just because they say so.

There are so many mysteries so much worth our time that are based in science it just seems foolish spending so much time reminiscing mythology. My Hope for the world is that we will awake to this realization of True over Fantasy and begin spending more time learning science over fairy tales, spend more time in Math over Superstition, Spend more time in Astronomy, Biology, Bio-Chemistry, Physics the Arts and culturally evolve to where we are not living under the disguise of mythological worship and Fear of letting go of the old world thinking and embracing the future of reason and science. Some scientist negate the existence of any higher power and I do disagree with this thinking because like I said before Synchronicity has been quite obvious in my life for example: Picking up the phone and the exact person you were thinking of is calling you or looking for a specific producer to take us from a local act to a national act and boom there they are. Life is Magical yet that magic is not based in some folklore or superstition it is based on the synchronicity of science, atomic molecules and the intelligence that lives within all things. Gawd is everywhere and in Everything Right under your nose, it is your nose.

Water is Known
by Many Names
All over the
World Yet it is still
Water, Such is the
Nature of Gawd...

The Folklore of
"LOVE"

Love and Romance, these are powerful forces in our reality. It seems everything and everyone is obsessed with this topic. "When will I find love, will I ever find love, can I love, am I loveable, will love ever find me, fuck love, do I love her, can I love him, my one true love, soul mates, I love you.."

I cannot speak for everyone yet I can speak from my own experience and I have sought love more than any other passion in my life and if trial and error is the litmus for science then I have been an active researcher for most my life with successes and failures. Yet like most of my old superstitious and mythological beliefs that I have shed like a skin I have discovered new Truths on the subject as well as False Premises that I have abandoned.

- Love is not some Destiny Event
- Love is not Selfish yet it is Self-First
- Love is a Choice

Love is not some destiny event that one particular soul mate has been picked out for us before we were here in this form. We are not destined to be with this person or that person. That overwhelming feeling inside of Crazy Love is a Chemical Reaction born into us over millions of years of species change that has given us the ability to adapt and prolong our genetic strain. I'm sorry; Love is not a movie or a story book. We find someone that makes us feel special because we see them as Beautiful and we Believe they represent something we deserve or sometimes more than we deserve and we feel special and then the Important part of the equation they accept us fully. This acceptance sends our "All In" genes that say this person loves me as much as I love them and now I can go all in and Trust them. That word Trust is not used enough, Love is thrown around quite a bit yet the word "Trust" is an even more Powerful Ethical trait than just the fondness for someone. My dog loves me without question yet to be understood by someone and even greater trait to actually Trust someone that they, you and your life can be invested with them for a long period of time or at least long enough to create the whole "Progeny Scenario", Kids, Home, Family a Life. One of our major factors to Real Love or a Love that can last is Trust. How do we develop Trust? Simple, don't fuck over your partner. It's that simple.

Love is not selfish yet it is Self- First. This means yes we must give, we must love, we must even give a little more sometimes yet if you do not stay focused on your own personal goals and passions you will only find a reason to resent your partner and end the relationship. Example:

MOM:-D

Mom gives and gives and gives and at the end of her day she feels empty or she feels like she has nothing left to give to her Man and the relationship suffers. Example:

Dad: -D

Dad works hard and earns $$ working hard and works hard some more, he neglects his passions, the life and the kids and the wife become about giving everything and getting nothing in return except complaints and bitching and seeks solace outside the relationship because that is the only place that gives something back

Seek Not to Be Selfish
But to BE SELF FIRST...

Love is a
CHOICE

Bottom Line we choose to get into shape. We realize that we don't feel good and that we don't look good and that when we see ourselves in the mirror we do not like ourselves very much and we get serious about Change. We buy all of the right equipment, we join the right gym, we find the right trainer, we listen and research the right advice, we buy the right food and take the right vitamins and we get serious about our commitment to our new schedule and the new you that will arise. It's Simple Right?

Love is the Same Way. We Choose to Love and to Be Loved In Return. We choose to defeat our self doubt and insecurities and we make the leap into the Great Cavern of Love and not an abyss. One can be navigated where one is a lost journey. We buy the right books, we attend the right meetings, we watch the right shows and YouTube videos, and you say, "What does this have to do about choosing love?" Well to Truly Love you have to first realize that you are broken, broken how? If you are even reading this you were meant too, if you are interested in what I am saying it is because Love has eluded you and the energy of synchronicity has lead you to my words. There are no accidents. We just have issues with seeing meaning in all of the synchronicity. My words say you are Broken and You are the mechanic, who else can be, who else is in charge of you except you, who else is man enough or woman enough for the job of fixing you than you? You will become a scientist and discover why you have pushed love away so many times. You say, "Me?" "It was her, and it was him." NO IT WAS YOU.

Now that we got that cleared up and I do apologize to your ego, no not really yet I do Hope you get what I'm saying You are in Charge of Fixing You.

Ok, you have done the work, you have seen the therapist, you have watched the videos, read the books and attended the seminars and now you're ready to "Be" with someone.

"It's a CHOICE"

After you have tasted the cornucopia of choices that are out there red head, brunette, blonde, Brazilian, model, singer, actress, country girl, milf, Asian, Black, Cuban, etc and then you realize, Wow what they look like isn't what I was going for at all, I want to feel good too!" Now I'm looking for a happy personality, positive personality, nurturer, homemaker, spiritually similar, family oriented, economic demographic similar, talks to me harshly the way mom did, speaks to me sweetly like dad did, pushes me like mom did, encourages me like dad did, disses me like dad did, do you see now we start trying to make something be something and that is the wrong way to look at this whole love game. Just Choose. Just Make a Commitment. Just Make a Choice and then do what every Great athlete knows from Michael Jordan to Randy Couture, Drill, Drill and Drill Some More! For you non athlete types, Keep

Doing, Going and Being About Your Choice. No matter what, Do not look for a Reason to Quit, Do not Just get mad, For once in your life make a choice and stick with it until you have discovered its end.

LOVE DOES NOT HAPPEN BY CHANCE IT IS HELD BY THOSE WHO HAVE THE COURAGE TO HOLD ONTO IT

Fighting Fears Takes You Everywhere

I remember my 1ˢᵗ phobia; I was walking thru the alleyway after getting dropped off from the bus in middle school. All of sudden out of nowhere a pit-bull had just taken a chunk out of my shin and three more just as big were right behind it. Instinctively I slammed my books I was carrying into its head and it released and turned around to go back in its yard and the other three followed. I hobbled into my yard to clean my leg and in that moment my fear of big dogs began. I was 14 years old and I was now extremely afraid of big dogs so much so I would run and hide in the bathroom if my friend brought his cute boxer over. This began a history of owning Big Beautiful Pit-Bulls. A Beautiful Majestic Strong Breed and its very True what they say they are like their owners so if you're an asshole chances are you own a Pitt that's overly aggressive and if your Kind and Patient he or she is probably a pussycat. Still All Powerful things must be handled with care. Remember Uncle Ben's quote to Peter Parker, "With Great Power Comes Great Responsibility." One day out of the blue or upon conscious awakening I realized that if it was between me and the dog it would have to be the dog. It was that simple and I was cured. I began to see that breed and all big dogs as just another misunderstood monster that just wanted to be loved. I adore them now. That was a dog, as I began to seek myself out I found that was not the only fear I had. There was the fear of water (Thanks Mom). My mother used to tell me when I was young that the dead who drowned had to pull someone under to take their place so they could leave. That's scary right, especially for a child. I then almost drowned once at Lake Ft. Phantom collecting shellfish with my mother. The stream I was walking thru suddenly became this roaring river emptying into the lake and having poor swimming skills this became quite the treacherous journey, at one time I looked up and realized I was four feet under the water and looking at the surface. Somehow miraculously I was washed to the shore before I reached the Deep Drop off into the lake; how I was saved I don't know. Then there was when I moved to South Florida and I was so excited to see the Ocean I didn't realize the rip current had pulled me in deeper than I was comfortable swimming. I start waving frantically at my friend David and he thought I was playing, waved back. He swam over to me and I held is britches and he dragged me back to shore. Then there was the time I took my two person kayak out for a midnight workout and my friend Jimmy

(I always thought how odd that his name was Jimmy too)

Tips over the kayak 2oo yards away from shore and without life jackets the kayak begins to sink. I immediately start swimming realizing 30 feet away I am not going to make it, even saying to Gawd in my head so this is how it ends, I decide to swim back and I tell jimmy I can't make the swim and with his help he saves my life and basically drags me back to shore. Completely exhausted I sit smiling while Jimmy can't believe what just happen and even accuses me of faking the whole thing to build up his self esteem because he had been feeling bad about leaving his hospitalized daughter in Chicago while he sought work in South Florida. He leaves and goes back to her the next day. It has always been funny to me how Americans will look at me like I'm some kind of Samurai Guide, their very Miyagi-San, Another Synchronistic event, I don't know. To say the least I was afraid of the water. I was very afraid. So what do I do? I buy a surfboard and decide I will conquer this fear just like the last. At first I just tie the leash to my ankle and float around on the board. Then a month later I am swimming around my board. Almost a year later I'm catching waves and I even surfed on the last Great Hurricane we had so yah I can swim and I am less afraid of the water yet one of the lessons and there are many the ocean teaches you and that is you will never beat her but you must respect her and I do. I am so pleased with conquering this fear because the exhilaration of Surfing, the pure Awesomeness of having the Ocean get behind you and push you forward is the closest thing I have ever felt to Gawds Hand Pushing Me Forward into Life.

Lean Forward Into Your Life

The original Fear for me was one of violence, violence in my home, violence in the street of North Crockett where I grew up in a predominantly Hispanic and African American Neighborhood. I still to this day remember with vivid clarity walking home from elementary and watching these two kids get off the middle school bus and duke it out at Jefferson and LaSalle and one boy began banging the head of the other kid up against the house and blood began gushing out of the kids head and everyone just cheered and roared as if they were in the stadium in a Gladiatorial Battle. It was life changing. I was like this life is rough and tough and you'd better be rough and tough to deal with it. From the pummeling the upper-class middle school kids would give the newbie's at every New Year. It was a terror to think that you had to take this beating and sometimes it was weekly until you joined the ranks of the eighth and ninth graders at Mann Middle School. Violence was all around me and I too had become violent fighting with the kids on my block and around my hood was a daily occurrence. Fighting in Abilene was just a common thing that we did at school, cruising North 1st & at Football games at parties just anywhere young people would gather.

Then I saw the Ultimate Fighting Championship in 1993 and 6 months later and a lot of beatings later at the local Judo, MMA School I found myself in my 1st 8 man tournament. No Gloves, No Weights and Fighters from All Over the World in what was the newest Freak show Blood Sport. I went undefeated from 1993-1997 Fighting for a World Title in the USWF sister show to Rings which eventually became Pride Fighting Championships. I didn't know it at the time because synchronistic paradigms were at work but I was being weaned from my Fear of Violence. I suffered a back fracture during my record label signing 2001-2006 that left me incapacitated for 6 months crawling to the bathroom and gaining over 40lbs while in bed rest. I then started a long 5 year process of getting back to normal. I knew at first to look for a holistic solution to my injury yet like most people I found myself in pain and desperate. The Medical Doctor I found after my M.R.I. identified me that I had a fracture in my L4 Region as well as herniated disc brought upon by years and years of repetitive high impact exercise. It was kind of humorous because the technician who did my MRI was married to one of the girls from the Robert Palmer video "Addicted to Love"; you know with the Hot models all playing instruments looking identical. I thought that was Cool. After turning down surgery several times and a year of Trigger Point injections in my back 15 at a time, I left the doctor's office and two hours later I returned still in excruciating pain. The doctor said there was nothing he could do if I wasn't down for surgery and gave me a flyer for a pain management clinic. I was like, "HELL NO!" South Florida is notorious for the free flowing pain medication and epidemic of pain addicts. I had no intention of becoming its next victim. Finally after a year of enigmatic quagmire I decide to look into a spiritual solution. I bought every book on back pain and healing. I sought out the best Chinese doctor and chiropractor and began a strict regimen of yoga 3 times a week. I dropped 40lbs thru walking and healthier eating habits. Pretty soon I was jogging and doing pushups and chin-ups at the local parks and 3 months later, NO MORE BACK PAIN. There was also a mental component I had to apply. A Great Book I recommend to everyone is, "You Can Heal Your Life" by Louise Hayes. In her book she has an entire section based on physical ailments and the mental connection between pain in the mind and the body.

Example:

The Back Represents your Column, Your Back Bone, Support System and Many times the Feeling of Lack of Support from your friends, family or co-workers cause "Stress" the "Life Killer" the "Well Being Killer" the Unease in your life and Mind that causes your Disease, Back Problems.

So after all this I returned to the training I had loved so much. I'm Obsessed with the Jiu Jitsu, Judo, Wrestling, Sparring, Muay Thai and Boxing. I have had such a passion for these arts my whole life. Little did I know it was an attempt to reach safety? I had to conquer the demons of my past the Fear of Violence. I chose the path of the Warrior to do so. There are many paths, that of the poet, the father, the mother, the dancer, the comedian and I had chosen the Warrior and at the same time had always walked the Path of the Entertainer, Singer/Songwriter mixed with sprinkles of Comedy. I am a multidimensional being.

So now I was training Fighters again and my friend James and I brought the 1st MMA (Mixed Martial Arts) Show to Abilene. A few years later I would begin fighting again at an age most say is too old to fight with a body that had already seen its prime. I was determined to prove myself again. I fought some of the toughest guys in the country in the South Florida Circuit which I believe is one of the Greatest MMA Hubs in the World because of the High Migration of Brazilians there. It was the Brazilians who birthed modern MMA Fighting in this manner for over 60 years before our 1st attempts at Vale Tudo (Anything Goes Fighting) I lost most my fights yet I had never felt so alive. I fought many times out of my weight category yet Victory was not the only question being asked I also needed to know I still could face violence chin to chin and Smile. I did many times. I also didn't realize how political and what a marketing tool the whole fight game was in South Florida. Being called in many times to fight heavier opponents just so they could rack up another win against someone they were certain to beat because of their weight advantage or preparation advantage. I didn't care though I had my own reasons for being in the cage this time around. I began to win, one of my friends commented to me one day you're on a two fight win streak and I thought who cares I'm here for the challenge. Promoters promised me fights against easy opponents and let me tell you in the world of MMA when two men are fighting in a cage like a dog there is no "Easy Fight" and I refused, it's not Samurai to look for Easy, I fought whomever was put in front of me and win or lose, out of my weight or not I fought them like a Man because I was no longer afraid of Violence. I fought 2x Brazilian Olympic Wrestler and Brazilian Jiu Jitsu Black Belt (BJJ) Renato Migliaccio; I fought undefeated fighters, XFC Champ Jarrod Card, UFC Fighter Mike Rio and UFC Fighter Raphael Rebello. Many top fighters many times out of my weight and once with one day notice. It had become a game, a game I had Won.

Osae Shinobu
Sharpen your
Sword
OSSU

When I was a
DRUG ADDICT

Wow what a party and the after party was even better than that. I remember my 1st roll, tab, X, E, XTC, and Ecstasy Pill. I was cheering at FAU in Boca Raton. Yes I was a college cheerleader and I will still Choke your ass out! Any who we decided to go to the ChiliePepper in Ft. Lauderdale and it was like Oz and I was the Tin Man. I was with our squad a smattering of Beautiful People and we were going to "roll" for the 1st time. I had never felt this feeling before MDMA (Methylenedioxymethylamphetamine) was the Drug and it was a drug that induced an extreme sense of well being and closeness. It could last anywhere from 3-6 hours and if taken in multitude you could roll for days. Often you would find yourself massaging one another because of the euphoric feeling of closeness and the inability to stop moving your hands. Lights would be more brilliant and the world would spin like a top. Combined with the other pharmaceuticals like GHB (Gamma Hydroxybutric Acid) an incredible intoxicant that one cap full can do what a bottle of Whiskey can do, Coke an upper that would make you move and shake like little Richard in his Hey Day, Mescaline Pills, Shroomies (Hallucinogenic Mushrooms) and to top it all off Nitrous (Nitrous Oxide or Laughing Gas) Tanks!! Now you have a party!! I mean the worlds we discovered! The parties that went for days at a time, traveling from apartment to apartment like we were traveling the Yellow Brickroad with fighters, club kids strippers dressed in over sized pants and crazy hats parading around from one apartment to the next, one Jacuzzi to the next. Oh the faces on the normal's when they would see us wondering around the lake side condos or pristine Boca housing developments talking to ducks and chasing each other around in the bushes and dragging G'd out (Passed Out) friends around like a weekend at Bernie's. It was a Magical time, Free Love and Non-Stop Celebration and then came along Special K (Meow) or Ketamine (A low grade animal tranquilizer that caused extreme hallucinations). Ketamine was Willywonka World on Steroids. It could be snorted and or injected and man what a ride! The world would begin to spin and the lights would become angels. One friend would always claim to hear angels singing when she was tripping K. I came close to what I believed was Gawds voice. I saw what looked like energy based angels that looked much like stingrays made out of light that would hover over our beds and watch over us. I once walked and talked to what Identified itself as the spirit of Gawd in Key west at Bartenders bash for over an hour which concluded in me stripping down naked and promising to follow what I thought was Gawd into a crowd of about 3,000 until my friends girlfriend ran out and covered me with a towel. Once I was celebrating my 28th birthday and one moment I was in the living room listening to music chilling on the couch and the next I was on a gurney somewhere with what looked like a reptilian doctor Identifying to the other reptilian technicians in the room that this one is awake and then I felt a shock to my heart, Boom I was back on the couch with my girl. Was any of this real? I do not know. What I do know is I was given a window into another reality that I had never seen before. A window that now almost 10 years sober I still am able to tap into Drug Free thru meditation and focus training. What is real? What we think? We all think so many different things. We believe we believe many things yet if we actually analyze the evidence of what we believe we find we do not know why we believe in all of the things we say we know. If someone is rationale enough to realize all they have been told is false will they humble themselves to question all that they think they know? Will they be courageous enough to question all they have been told and taught? I do not know. I do not care. We are each our own responsibilities and it is not our duty to convert others to our way of thinking. This is something the fearful do to convince themselves what they believe is True. Righteousness is best felt in numbers. Of course %99 of the world once thought that the world was flat, that did not make it so. My favorite podcast the Joe Rogan Experience often comments what can seriously be gained by discussing anything with anyone who has never tripped the universe, it's as if the conversation cannot continue because what would an Physicist have to say to a Neanderthal. I am being dramatic yet you get my drift. Have you ever had a conversation with true blue bible thumper that could not, would not hear anything you had to say and only used their mythology book which they have had little knowledge of where and how the book was pieced together by the Roman Emperor Augustine to serve the empire not mankind? Or constantly used the word "Faith" as there answer for everything they don't know which tends to be a lot & when asked why they just keep reiterating you have to have faith? Well I can't just have faith. There are reasons for all things. There are answers of how the Universe came into being and who we are and what our purpose here is.

In the 1800's the Chinese witnessed and recorded a bright light in the sky that lasted for over 30 days. It was a Super Nova or a dying star that becomes a black hole and releases a burst of energy greater than all of the energy in our universe. It has since been witnessed and recorded as becoming a new galaxy known as the Crab Nebula. Our galaxy much like this one came into being in the same manner. Approximately 30-40 planets once occupied our newly forming sun and thru cohesion (the sticking together of space debris) and gravity became the nine or 8 planets we have now depending on who you ask. Asteroids delivered materials like water and the biochemistry components and life began here on our planet. We are a result of that. It is thought that we are the only planet that holds life yet in May of 2012 over 200 light years away a planet has been discovered within the safe zone of its suns solar system with the same climate as earth now isn't that something! You are the result of millions of years of evolution. The discovery of fire, brain larger, hunting for meat, brain larger, the use of tools, brain larger, hunting and gathering, brain larger, killing off the Neanderthal killing weaker strains of humanoids, brain larger, modern medicine, brain larger, TV, books, art, science, larger, Larger and LARGER. This is who we are.

Finally your purpose here:

Is what you say it is. Move toward that which you Love, Not that which you can tolerate, like most people do. Move toward that which inspires you.

Move toward that which drives you to passion.

Just Do You and Be Yourself.

I like most people spent some part of my life wondering what I was meant to do. I worked every job under the sun and actually under the sun those jobs always sucked. I worked in an office, on television, for television, in a restaurant, bar, construction, security, recreation management and the only job I ever had any luck maintaining was teaching and entertaining. I still let go of those two passions to seek "real employment" usually for woman who cared more about material things than in the happiness of their partner. Yet I realized one day what I loved and it was what I had always loved to do. Play and Entertain people. I remember my 7th grade Biology teacher Mrs. Purkis who would give me the last 5 minutes of every class to get up and entertain everybody and I loved it! I have always been a competitor or someone who loves to play games. I had been competing in gymnastics heavily since I was 9 years old, then it was bodybuilding, then fighting and so on. Every day in the dojo I am able to compete with my younger and stronger students building my business and exercising my love of athletic competition & every time I get on stage I am able to share new material, old favorites, joke and tell stories from my life and observations of life. I am in Heaven Because I have all that I need doing all that I Love. I do not believe in the Devil. I do not believe in hell. We can create hellish circumstances to live within for a time yet no metaphorical flames and pitchforks. I do believe in a creator that creates using the physics it created and Heaven is here on Earth. Doing What You Love with Who You Love is Glorious! If you've ever been fortunate enough to see Joseph Cambell on PBS passionately pontificating about the myths of old, you were blessed to hear stories of the Greeks, Arthurian Legend, the Egyptians and just about every culture that ever existed. His repertoire of ancient cultures was legendary yet what I found most exhilarating about him was the way he could tie these old stories into morals for today. Often he would talk about the rights of passage for a young man. The rituals of a particular tribe or culture that would put a boy thru some test of passage, in the movie 300 we see the young Leonidas hunting and killing a wolf which ushered him in to manhood. Today we have lost many of our cultural rights of passage yet in some homes there is still taught the skill of hunting and gathering which some find barbaric yet I find it to be a necessity to life and to your family. It's arrogant and foolish to believe that the government will always be able to provide food for you and your family. These acts of teaching your children to hunt have become some of our own examples of rites of passage. This simplicity in living is part of that Heaven I speak of. Returning to simple things and distancing of yourself from a technological driven world can add to the Heaven of your creation. Joseph Cambell knew that we could learn from the ancients on how to live today. We often find ourselves caught up in such futile things like becoming great or doing something of magnificent proportions just to feed our ego and insecurity of being somebody of worth. We hustle around pressuring others to do the same. We are always in a hurry. We are always griping about people and their performance because we believe it is not up to our standard. We must only be concerned about our own standard. We must stop focusing so much on cultural competition between family members or friends or acquaintances and just focus on simplicity, ethics and Happiness. Happiness is Bliss. Bliss is Success. Do not seek to be great, it is better to be good. A great man wears a heavy crown of burden. A good man is Happy and Blissful All the Days of his Life.

Follow Your Bliss – Joseph Cambell

I See Gawd Here Too

There is intelligence or another way to see Gawd because to me Gawd is this intelligence in all things from the organ to the cell to the atom to the subatomic particle. Within the sub-atomic particle we see the promotion of life, survival, replication, consciousness, function, form, connection, etc this is another form of the Gawd Label.

Within the molecule we see the promotion of life, survival, replication, consciousness, function, form, connection, etc this is another form of the Gawd Label.

Within the Stem Cell we see the promotion of life, survival, replication, consciousness, function, form, connection, etc this is another form of the Gawd Label.

And so on and so forth...

If we are the cue ball are we playing a game of our choosing can we influence our development, can we evolve and change by will alone the same way we win our pool game. I know that at the age of 28 and feeling broken with a broken spirit and fractured back I was becoming someone I did not want to be and thru synchronistic events and sure will power I changed all of that and now I am a much younger man in my 40 year old body than I was at 28. People all the time remark on my age and how I look from my skin to my shape to my bones to my zest for life is this just coincident or have I manipulated matter and space and time? I feel in touch with who I am and what I am. I actively support my belief system with affirmation therapy. A Deep Study and Constant meditation on the things I know increase my vitality and sense of well being. There is a formula for balanced and joyful life and that formula can sound like this:

1 Cup Physical Activity

1 Cup Mental Study in the Sciences and Positive Self Help

1 Cup Focusing on Being Self First at the Same Time Learning to Value and Enjoy People

1 Cup of Actively Experiencing Your Passion

1 Cup of a Loving Relationship

Gawd is in you because all of these things, subatomic particles, atoms, cells, organs and the intelligence that makes up all of this are you and therefore the Gawd in which I speak of is you. At times your are conscious of this fact when everything is going extremely well and at times you are blind to this fact when things aren't going so well yet it is always within your ability to call upon this Gawdhood and this intelligence. How can you call upon your Gawdhood? You can call upon your Gawdhood in much the same way you prepare yourself for combat or make a sandwich you focus on it. You deliberately place your attention on your Gawdhood your ability to promote life, survival, replication, consciousness, function, form, connection, etc this is another form of the Gawd Label. Often I will close my eyes and center myself by breathing deeply in my nose and out of my mouth ten times focusing on the sound of my breath. Then once I have centered myself or cleared my mind of distraction I focus my mind on what it is I wish to Gawd and that becomes my Result on Gawding in that moment.

I am Gawd

The Law Of Attraction Or As I See It The Way I Set My Mind On Getting Stuff Done

About ten years ago I saw the video the secret. Like most people I had never heard of this topic and was fascinated by the concept that putting myself in the right vibrational feeling I could hasten my fondest desire into my reality.

This was much easier said than done yet I personally found that what I was addressing in the beginning was my general negative outlook on the world. I always acted as if I was Happy or pretended to be happy yet that was not the same thing as Truly becoming a positive person who always saw the world as half full instead of half empty. At first I found that I was a slave to my mind and my entire negative mind chapter. It took me many years to silence the negative persistent voice that was in my head.

You are Not Your Thoughts.

In the movie Peaceful Warrior a book by Dan Millman the character Socrates tells Dan an impatient ego driven young man, "YOU ARE NOT YOUR THOUGHTS." We are not the repetitive mind chatter that goes on all day in our head. We are so much more. We are Eternal Energy and Information. (EEI)

How do we do these things? I will give you a clue yet my intention is to go into more depth in my next chronicle. One technique that I teach all of my students is the Ten Second Meditation.

- 1ˢᵗ Sit Comfortably
- 2ⁿᵈ Close Your Eyes
- Breathe Deeply, Slowly Into Your Mouth and Out of Your Mouth
- Focus on the Sound of Your Breath
- For Ten Seconds Straight Do Only That Until You Can Focus Only On the Sound of Your Breath for a Total of Ten Seconds

This sounds easy yet can be difficult at 1ˢᵗ. Continue Practicing until you can do 10 seconds, 30 seconds, 1 minute and so on. Eventually you will be able to meditate for extended periods and then you will be ready for the next phase.

This meditation provides Peace in times of Stress. This meditation is the 1ˢᵗ tool in manifesting the right "Vibration" or "State of Mind or Being" for attaining your goals.

After you have began to clear your mind of negative chatter you will find that you feel lighter, happier and are more able to focus on the things you want to manifest in your life. I always tell the girls, "When you're looking for something in your room, turn the lights on 1ˢᵗ. Clearing the mind of chatter, "Turns on the Lights in Your Room."

When the lights are on it is much easier to find what you are looking for.

The Right Tool for the Job

Since I was a child I have always been amazed by the sound a guitar can make. I have owned crappy guitars and I have owned magical guitars. Having the right guitar can make all the difference on stage. An in tune guitar sounds like Angel Choirs an Out of tune guitar can ruin a show. When you wish to become an Award Winning Singer-Songwriter which I am, you have to have the right tools for the job. Do not expect to become a Pianist and not own a piano. Your "Attraction or Manifestation" Needs the right tools for the job. A Fighter Needs a Good Trainer. A business man needs capitol and great idea. A Pizza Shop needs dough.

A Guide

When attracting an outcome it is best to ask for or seek out a guide. A guide can come in many forms and I cannot really tell you what your guide will be. A guide will manifest along your journey in a natural way. Seek and ye shall find. There are guides everyday that will point you in the right direction toward your goal. You only have to be willing to open your eyes and heart and hear them. Do not be concerned for where they will come from or if they will come, just know with certainty that they will.

Courage

Last yet not least, you must be courageous. Often you will feel you are at a lost. You feel worry where will this come from or how you will get capitol for your ideas yet if you move forward and have a knowing that all will come together it will. The courage to take a chance and experiment is all that it is needed.

The Sun and What Might Happen
When You Die

For many years we did not know that the Sun was star. Newton hypothesized that the stars were far away suns. How did the Greatest scientist of all time figure this out nearly 300 years ago? I have always felt special kindred relationship to our Sun. When you think about how often people throw around the word God and yet completely ignore the fact that the Sun, our Sun is Everything to us. It is heat, it is light and it is Life. Without our Sun there is no us. I have for sometime practiced Sun meditation where I stare directly into the sun and meditate. People will say not to do this yet I can still see and I feel something profound when I do this special Sun Meditation. I also feel an ongoing dialogue and if we people were to ever show thanks and praise and reverence for anything in our solar system how can we not praise the Sun how can we not see that itself has identity. The ancient Egyptians worshiped the Sun as Ra and The Greeks as Apollo and I thank the Sun everyday for its gift of love, light and life for us all. We often pray for miracles or for Gawd to give us a sign of its existence and what Greater miracle exists in our reality or solar system than our own sun. The Nebula of cosmic gases and elements that make up the Sun came 1st in our solar system and in its violent origin birthed our solar system and within its guidance formed our planets and controls the gravitational pull and cycle of orbit within our Milky Way galaxy which will collide with Andromeda galaxy in a few billion years and then what. I also believe that the Suns/ Stars act as synapse in the body relaying energetic charges from one solar system to the next and from one galaxy to another. This is where I begin my speculation yet every major religion in the world hypothesizes on all kinds of things so here goes my turn.

Why would Stars relay from one to another thru out the Universe? Easy, that's how we or our (Souls) travel. The Eternal Energy and Information that makes up the Eternal You is Light. We are light. Now to tell you what happens when we die. Gravity is one of the Fundamental Forces that shape our Reality. There is Gravity, Electromagnetism, Strong and Weak Nuclear Force. The Sun Projects light and life at our planet and from this light, from this radiation, energy that comes from the Sun everything we know exists on planet earth. Therefore when we die when the gravity of our own bodies can no longer contain our (Eternal Energy and Information) (EEI) the next Greatest source of Gravity in our Solar System comes into play and we are zipped away at light speed to the SUN. Einstein theorized that the gravity of the Sun shaped and warped the space and time around planets and Comets that passed Stars. This has been proven thru cosmology. Our Spirits being of Free Will then can choose to go or be wherever and whenever it chooses because light does not act in the same manner as physical matter. Light has no bounds when it comes to time and space yet it does use a method and it does travel the intergalactic super highway. So where do all the Souls go, well that's a mystery for another book.

There are mysteries from the past
That are no longer mysteries at all,
The same will be said of the mysteries of today

The Quantum Gawd

Dr. Richard Dawkins Biologist and leading voice in the non-theist movement or atheist movement believes there is no evidence for god. I believe part of the issue here is trying to replace one mythological creator with another. We have replaced the Egyptian god Ra, with the Greek god Zeus, with the Jewish god Yahweh and now the prevalent god of the Christians Jesus Christ. Dawkins now can't see any reason to replace Christ with another mythological creator and I can understand why. However I feel the Real god, the god who is right under his nose, which is measurable and full of evidence, is the Quantum Gawd. Within the cell and beyond that at the sub-atomic level is the atom with its form, function, directive, replication and basically life. Life is building itself toward life's ultimate goal? The ultimate goal is to "be." Life has an intention to exist. Life has an intention to create. Life has an intention to replicate itself, or in other words give off progeny. I believe within this subatomic level there is evidence for Gawd. I believe now with the invention of the subatomic microscope we are witnessing Gawd, Gawding. Gawd is being Gawd. Unlocking the secrets or science of this subatomic field could release potential that we have only dreamed of. Einstein equation $E=MC2$ unlocked the Atomic Bomb and Atomic Energy. Whose to say that we will not unlock the ability create magnetic fields around our bodies and heal ourselves, transport ourselves at the speed of light, fly by reversing our magnetic charge? The possibilities are endless. Gawd is a measurable, knowable, evidential property that exists in the quantum world.

GAWD IS A QUANTUM GAWD

By Professor Jimmy "Ninja" Chaikong

Dedicated to my Family

Via MMA Analyst Jen Boronico
You sir, are a pioneer. You talked the talk and walked the walk decades before anyone else. Now the masses find the "pot of gold", but Jim chaikong was one of the first to discover it, master it and teach it. #respect

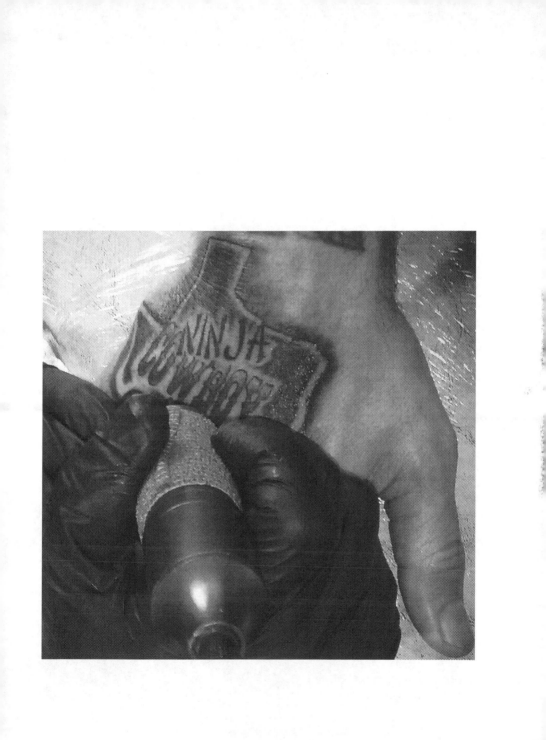

Printed in the United States
by Baker & Taylor Publisher Services